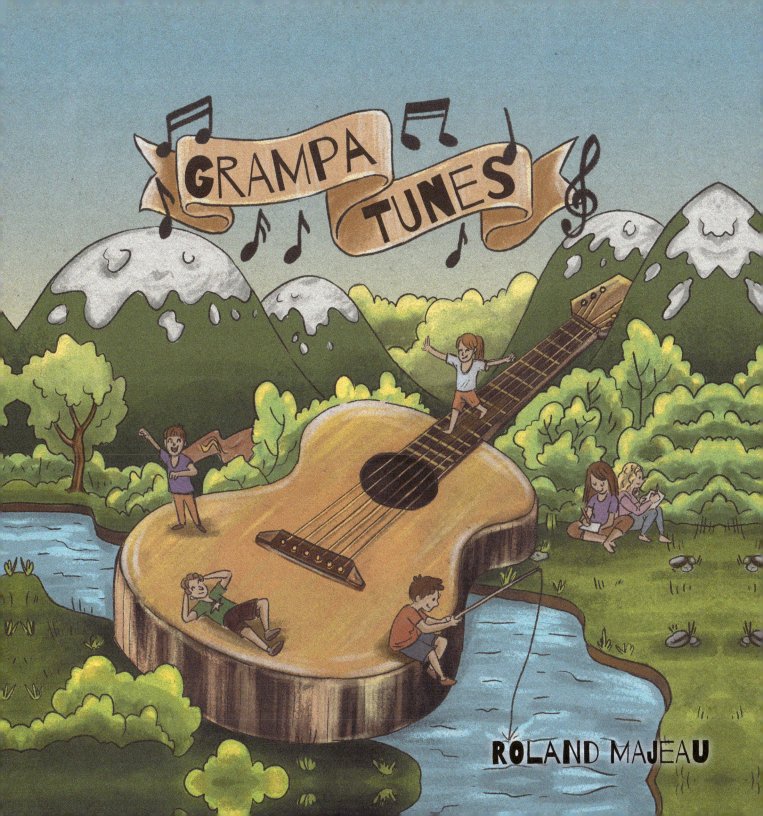

With the birth of each grandchild,
a song was written.

A song to impart some Grampa-like wisdom.
(If there is such a thing.)

This advice is not just for those children,
but the adults they become as well.

Here we are with the first five amazing grandkids.
These are their songs.

Grampa Tunes.
The book for *everyone*, not just the grandkids.

*Charlotte, you have given me unwavering support
and encouragement, this book would not have been possible
without you. Thank you.*

Journey Round the Sun

You and I have this common ground,
we both are traveling round and round.

On this rock, that's what us people do.
We've seen it many times,
I know it's new for you.

And we'll explore it as we journey
around the sun.

We find adventure!
We'll see what treasures lie ahead!

And hand in hand, we'll take your first trip
around the sun.

So tell your friends, your dad, your mom
that you heard this from your Grampa:

"Life is great, and life is fine,
and love will conquer every time."

As we take our trips around the sun.
As we journey all around the sun.

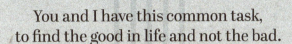

You and I have this common task,
to find the good in life and not the bad.

On this rock, that's what us people do.
We've seen it many times,
and we can show it to you.

And we'll explore it as we journey
around the sun.

We find adventure!
We'll see what treasures lie ahead!

And hand in hand, we take another trip
around the sun.

So tell your friends, your dad, your mom
that you heard this from your Grampa:

"Life is great, and life is fine,
and love will conquer every time."

As we take our trips around the sun.
As we take our trips around the sun.

As we journey all around the sun, the sun.
Take our trips around the sun, the sun.
Journey all around,
take our trips around,
journey all around . . . the sun.

Composed for Martin.

GRAMPA LOVES YOU!

HELP US BELIEVE

In all my life, I've told myself
it's better to believe.
That there's good inside most everyone,
sometimes it's hard to see.

In all my life, I've seen some things
so hard to comprehend.
But with you now born into our world,
I'm stronger till the end.

Help me to see the things I need to see
when I'm blinded by the pain.

Help me to hear the things I need to hear,
like laughter every day.

Oh, grandchild, you help me to believe.

Help me believe that superheroes win
when they're fighting for what's right.

Help me to find the hero that I need
inside of my own life.

Oh, grandchild, you help me to believe!

In all my life, I've told myself
persistence is the way.
If you don't give up and don't give in,
you'll make a better place.

In all my life, I've seen some mountains
stubborn till the end.
But it's childlike faith that moves those mountains
put in place by man.

Help us to see the things we need to see
when we're blinded by the pain.

Help us to hear the things we need to hear,
like laughter every day.

Oh, grandchild, you help us to believe.

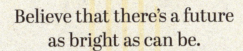

Believe that there's a future
as bright as can be.

And believe that it's a good thing
if we all believe in dreams.

Help us believe that superheroes win
when they're fighting for what's right.

Help us to find the heroes that we need
inside of our own lives.

Oh, grandchild, you help us to believe.

Oh, grandchild, you help us to believe!

You help us to believe.
You help us to believe.

Help us to believe!

Composed for Henry.
GRAMPA LOVES YOU!

Early in the morning,
when you wake up from your bed,
toys are scattered on the floor,
dreams are building in your head.

You're starting on a journey,
and you'll take it step by step.

You're growing, and you're learning,
and there's something that I'd like to share:

Remember your prayers.
Remember your friends.
Remember when you're troubled,
or you're blue.

Remember,
Mom and Dad are here for you.

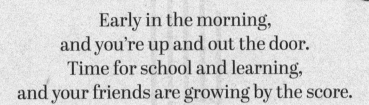

Early in the morning,
and you're up and out the door.
Time for school and learning,
and your friends are growing by the score.

You're traveling on your journey,
and there's freedom in the air.

You're on the way, you're on your own.
There's something that I'd like to share:

Remember your prayers.
Remember your friends.
Remember when you're troubled,
or you're blue.

Remember,
Gram and Gramps are here for you.

So, on you'll grow, and we'll be there.
Time flies by, I know.

So, on you'll grow, and we'll be there.
To see you shine so bright, I know.

Early in the morning,
and you'll hear a happy tone.
Voices of the ones you love
fill the place you call your home.

You are now the grown-up,
and you make the world go round.

Somewhere in your busy life,
I hope that you can hear the sound.

Remember your prayers.
Remember your friends.
Remember when you're troubled,
or you're blue.

Remember, Mom and Dad are here.
Remember, Gram and Gramps are here.
Remember that your family's here for you.

Composed for Timothy.

GRAMPA LOVES YOU!

One day, you'll walk with me.
Maybe with the sun so bright,
maybe on a rainy night,
or one day with the snow upon the ground.

One day, you'll talk to me.
Little words at first, I know.
Give it time, and they will grow.
One day I know you could lecture me.

These are the dreams that I have for you.
Many dreams in your life will come true.
Great are the things that I know you will do.

Count on us, we all believe in you!

One day, you'll write to me.
Maybe with a paper note,
maybe on some new tech phone,
or maybe something else to say hello.

These are the dreams that I have for you.
Many dreams in your life will come true.
Great are the things that I know you will do.

Count on us, we all believe!

Wonders of the world,
mysteries unfold.

Starry skies and ocean tides
leave me all spellbound.

Still, I dream . . .

One day, you'll think of me.
Think of how we joked around.
Think, and you can laugh out loud.
But when you think of me,
I hope you're proud.

These are the dreams that I have for you.
Many dreams in your life will come true.
Great are the things that I know you will do.

Count on us, we all believe.
Count on us, we all believe.
Count on us, we all believe . . . in you!

Composed for Britton.

GRAMPA LOVES YOU!

SMILE

Some say
a smile is straight from heaven,
and I kind of think they're right.

Some say
that laughter is good medicine.
If you take it, you'll be alright.

So, if you can smile and you can laugh,
no telling where it will lead.

Will you take this chance?
Will you take this chance with me?

Some say
believing makes a difference,
even if the odds are all against you.

Some say
That hope will give you courage
for the hard things you've got to do.

So, if you believe and you have hope,
no telling where it will lead.

Will you take this chance?
Will you take this chance with me?

Some say
that kindness is a virtue.
I know it helps us all get along.

Some say
that friendship is a fortress,
a place to keep you from harm.

So, if we are kind and we are friends,
no telling where it will lead.

Will you take this chance?
Will you take this chance with me?

Some say
a smile is straight from heaven,
and I kind of think they're right.

Composed for Annika.

GRAMPA LOVES YOU!

Rachael and Her Satchel

Rachael has a satchel
that she carries
on her shoulder,
and she walks out on the water,
and her feet are getting colder.

She struggles over pebbles
to get back to the shore.

Rachael doesn't walk there anymore.

Rachael has a football
in the satchel
on her shoulder,
and she kicked it in the meadow
that she thought was only clover.

She found it full of thistles,
it made her bare feet sore.

Rachael doesn't kick there anymore.

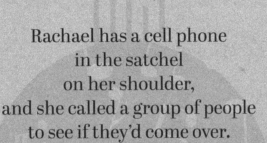

Rachael has a cell phone
in the satchel
on her shoulder,
and she called a group of people
to see if they'd come over.

No one came to visit
as she waited by the door.

Rachael doesn't call them anymore.

Rachael has a notebook
in the satchel
on her shoulder,
and she took a pen to write a note
to say that it's all over.

Then suddenly, from nowhere,
appeared a long-time friend.

She said, "Rachael, put away the pen."

Rachael has a satchel
that she carries
on her shoulder,
and she walks out on the water,
and her feet are getting colder.

She struggles over pebbles
to get back to the shore.

But Rachael has been walking even more.

Rachael has a football
in the satchel
on her shoulder,
and she kicked it in the meadow
that she knew was not just clover.

She knew the damn thistles
would make her bare feet sore.

Rachael has been kicking even more.

Rachael has a cell phone
in the satchel
on her shoulder.
She called a group of people
to see if they'd come over.

Many came to visit,
they were knocking on her door.

Rachael has been calling even more.

Rachael has a notebook
in the satchel
on her shoulder,
and she took a pen to write a note
to say that it's not over.

She wrote.

Because of friendship,
her life has been restored.

Rachael has been writing even more.

Rachael has a satchel
that she carries
on her shoulder,
and she walks out on the water,
and her feet are getting colder.

She's dancing over pebbles
and running on the shore.

Rachael is in love with life once more.

Composed for everyone.
WE ALL NEED HOPE AND ENCOURAGEMENT!

ABOUT THE AUTHOR

Roland Majeau started writing songs at the age of fourteen and has recorded six full albums and several singles since then. He hopes that his healing messages are carried through his music to the ears that need to hear them. He has written hundreds of songs, and the ones inside this book are some of his favourites.

Roland lives with his wife, Charlotte, in Edmonton, Alberta.

One Printers Way
Altona, MB R0G 0B0
Canada

www.friesenpress.com

Copyright © 2022 by Roland Majeau
First Edition — 2022

Illustrator: Pranisha Shrestha

All rights reserved.

No part of this publication may be reproduced in any form, or by any means, electronic or mechanical, including photocopying, recording, or any information browsing, storage, or retrieval system, without permission in writing from FriesenPress.

ISBN
978-1-03-910658-1 (Hardcover)
978-1-03-910657-4 (Paperback)
978-1-03-910659-8 (eBook)

1. JUVENILE NONFICTION, MUSIC

Distributed to the trade by The Ingram Book Company

CPSIA information can be obtained
at www.ICGtesting.com
Printed in the USA
BVHW021120120722
641924BV00008B/638